I M A G E S

Toys

Karen Bryant-Mole

Heinemann

First published in Great Britain by Heinemann Library, Halley Court, Jordan Hill, Oxford OX2 8EJ, a division of Reed Educational & Professional Publishing Ltd.

OXFORD FLORENCE PRAGUE MADRID ATHENS MELBOURNE AUCKLAND KUALA LUMPUR SINGAPORE TOKYO IBADAN NAIROBI KAMPALA JOHANNESBURG GABORONE PORTSMOUTH NH (USA) CHICAGO MEXICO CITY SAO PAULO

Designed by Jean Wheeler
Commissioned photography by Zul Mukhida
Produced by Mandarin Offset Ltd.
Printed and bound in China

01 00 99 98 97
10 9 8 7 6 5 4 3 2 1

ISBN 0 431 06304 4

British Library Cataloguing in Publication Data
Bryant-Mole, Karen
Toys. - (Images)
1.Toys - Juvenile literature 2.Readers (Primary)
I.Title
688.7'2

Some of the more difficult words in this book are explained in the glossary.

Acknowledgements
The Publishers would like to thank the following for permission to reproduce photographs.
Eye Ubiquitous; 8 (left), Tony Stone Images; 23 (right) Andre Perlstein, Zefa; 8 (right), 9 (left and back cover), 9 (right), 22 (both), 23 (left).

Every effort has been made to contact copyright holders of any material reproduced in this book. Any omissions will be rectified in subsequent printings if notice is given to the Publisher.

Contents

Materials

Toys can be made from different **materials**.

These **vehicles** are made from wood.

These animals are
made from plastic.

Texture

The word 'texture' means how something feels.

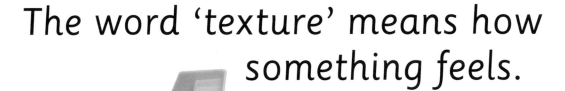

These toys feel hard.

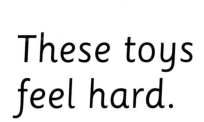

These toys feel soft.

Wheels

All of these toys have wheels.

You can travel quickly
on toys with wheels.

Moving toys

How would you make these toys move?

pull

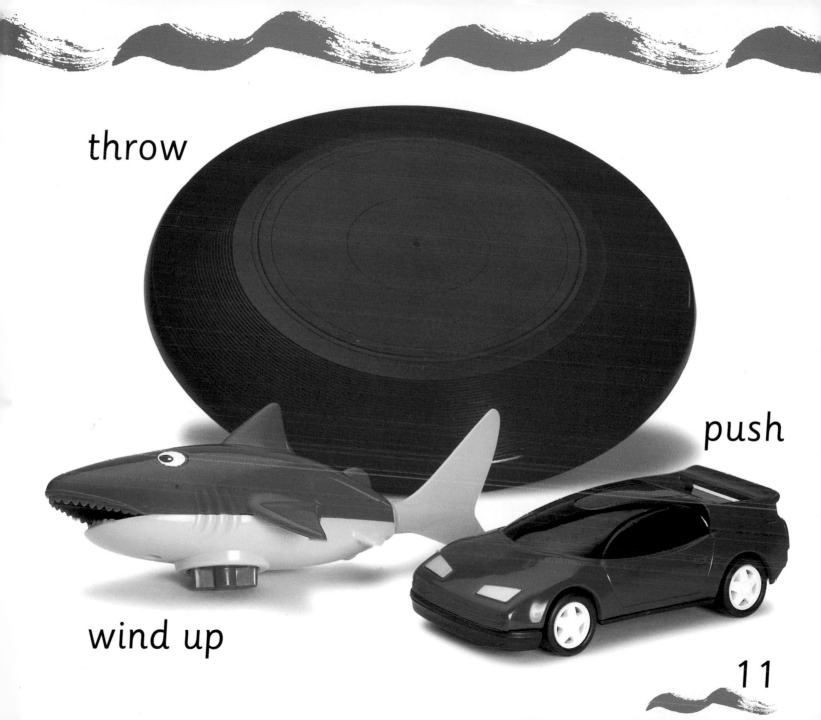

throw

push

wind up

11

Batteries

These toys need batteries to make them work.

Toys with batteries
have switches, so that they
can be turned on and off.

Noisy toys

These toys make different types of sounds.

They are
all toy
musical
instruments.

Some toys can be used
to build or make things.

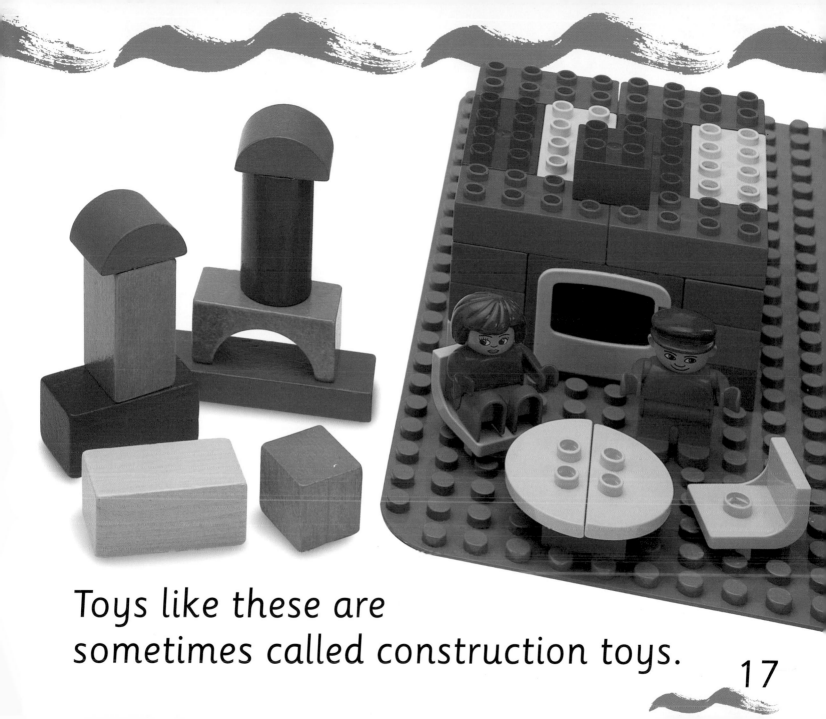

Toys like these are
sometimes called construction toys.

Jigsaw puzzles

Jigsaw puzzles can
be easy or difficult.

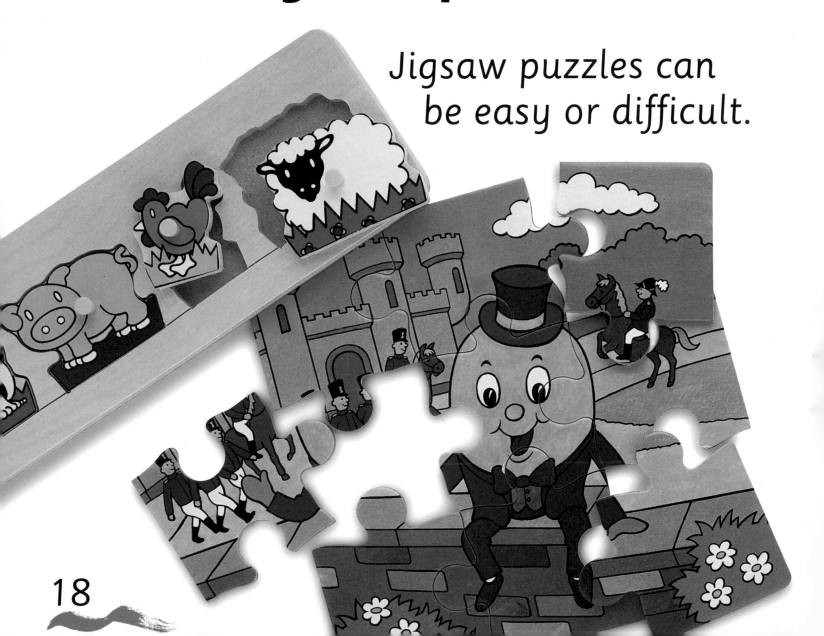

Which of these
puzzles looks the easiest?

Pretend play

These toys are pretend **versions** of things that we have at home.

iron

toaster

food

telephone

21

Outdoor toys

Some toys are usually played with outdoors.

play house

bouncer

kite

bucket and spade

Glossary

batteries objects that store electricity and can be used to make things work

materials what things are made from

musical instruments things that you can make music with

vehicles things that move people or objects from place to place

version something that is like something else

Index